JUST BELIEVE

Reasons Why Your Faith Matter

Robert H. Marshall Jr.

TABLE OF CONTENTS

Foreword

Dr. John Veal

Hebrews 11:1 tells us that faith is the substance of things hoped for and the evidence of things not seen. The Greek word for "substance" used in this particular verse is Hupostasis. Hupo meaning "stand" and stasis interpreted as "under". When put together, it's defined as "that which stands under, a foundation, undergirds, or support." It also implies the grounds on which one builds hope, that which underlies what is apparent, reality, or a "title deed." Essentially, faith is a title deed to answered prayer, or things hoped for. Faith is a doorway into the reality of God's voice. Faith is believing before you see. It's walking in the will of God without seeing your final destination. Faith is about trusting Him, taking His hand and allowing the Lord to lead you.

In Robert Marshall's book, Just Believe, he takes you on an odyssey during which various levels of faith are addressed and thoroughly explained. He lavishly uses quotes from a myriad of pioneers in Christian ministry, the political arena and the marketplace. His writings have a scholarly feel to them and they will challenge your very understanding of your personal walk of faith. Scripture is used generously, providing the framework and foundation of each chapter of this manuscript. The author prompts the reader to examine his or her notion of what faith really is by providing thought-provoking examples from his own life experiences. I believe that the addition of real-world situations brings more flavor to his writings. It makes this book unique and gives it a stand-alone quality. There are many books that have been written on the subject and Marshall's work is not a regurgitation of any of them. Robert's manuscript is fresh and meant as a welcome addition to faith's vast literary library.

Marshall is a gifted writer, who pays attention to detail and keeps his readers in mind. I love his child-like faith that he speaks about in the beginning of the book, believing that anything is possible with God! The wonderment that Robert illustrates here should be the kind of faith utilized well into adulthood. This is key to getting what you want from the Lord. He knows this and it's quite evident that Marshall wants you to grasp it as well.

His transparency throughout is both a rarity and a strength. This attribute makes his book more relatable and reader friendly. You feel as if you're privy to the inner-most thoughts and views on subject matter that is immensely meaningful to Robert. It's evident in the effort that he takes to make the complex simple and easy to comprehend. In the years I've known Robert, he's always come across as someone that values family, people and excellence. This is apparent in every endeavor that he embarks upon. I highly recommend not only purchasing this book, but also suggesting it to others that want their faith to go to another level. I believe the tenets and concepts within this manuscript will be referred back to often. As you read it, be prepared for a re-igniting of the faith to believe God for the impossible.

-Dr. John Veal
Author of "Supernaturally Prophetic: A Practical Guide for Prophets & Prophetic People" and "Supernaturally Delivered: A Practical Guide to Deliverance & Spiritual Warfare"
Johnveal.org

Endorsements

In today's culture, many face terminal diseases and illnesses that plague our nation. However, I believe we have a greater dilemma on our hands. We have a plague, a parasite that consumes the inner-man of its hope and love and joy. We have a symbiont that aims to attach itself to the soul of every human being and that venom is called un-forgiveness. Whenever we practice un-forgiveness we are moving and living in ritual fear. Faith moves us to embrace both forgiveness and restoration. The goal in life is to allow faith to become the compass that leads us. I encourage those whom may struggle in their walk of faith, their trust in God, their belief in themselves to read this book. Just believe unveils the anatomy of a true believer in the 21st century. May your life never be the same after this book.

-Louis Wimbley
CEO, Louis Wimbley Global Ministries Inc.
Chicago, IL

In the book "Just Believe", Robert Marshall is transparent and truthful to his experiences in life! What he shares in this book is personal and although his life experiences are painful he leads the reader on a course that acknowledges the "agonies of life" as humans as he takes them to a place in God where healing and deliverance resides! In this book

Robert allows the reader to be human yet his approach to mending from "human hurts" is spiritual! Truly this book will serve as a "self-help" to many!

-Dr. Sharon R. Peters
Founder, Sweet Rose of Sharon
Women's Ministry

Robert Marshall, has written some practical approaches that are packed with so much "must read information". As you pick up these principles of empowerment, they will assist you in maturing your Faith to handle life's issues that seem impossible. You will not want to put this book down once you start reading it. It's transformative, with life examples with daily application that will instruct you, enlighten you, and make you laugh, cry, love and live!

-Bishop Anthony Hatcher
Senior Pastor of Faith Life Outreach Christian Cathedral

The pages are riveting with transparency and honesty; you can actually feel the healing hands maneuvering your misunderstandings and removing your unforgiveness as the writer processes through the pain, right on the pages. The scripture references are made relevant bringing life to ancient scriptural events that are made clear through current practical situations. This is a must read as the writer, honesty, the scriptures and therapy hold hands with you to lead you to total recovery.

-Edwin A Newsome D.D.
Founder and Pastor, Kingdom Impact Church

Just Believe is not a typical book about faith. Robert does an amazing job drawing from his personal experiences and takes you through a journey with him that not only makes you want to know more "things" about God, but makes you desire a deeper, more intimate relationship with God. As you read this book, be open and prepare yourself for an amazing ride that is sure to spark a new passion within you to deepen your faith.

-Isaac Watson
Founder and Senior Leader, Encounter Worship Center
Author of Access Granted: Unlocking Your Potential as an Intercessor

Forgiveness has to be one of the most touchiest of conversations; the subject, itself, takes on a complex life of its own and can morph into different forms of emotions and expressions within different people at different times for different reasons. In 'Just Believe', Author, Robert Marshall Jr., spares no expense 'going there' and impressively manages to candidly, clearly, contextually, compassionately and carefully minister to matters of the heart without ever losing connection with The Heart of The Master concerning FORGIVENESS. This book is drenched with soul stirring insights and life application exercises that will help you grow through stagnate places.

-LeRon Atkinson
Social Media Influencer & Philanthropist, Author

I would like to dedicate this book to my amazing family. My wife Jacqueline Marshall and our 3 amazing children, Caleb, Caden, and Ariyah. I look at you all in awe struck wonder and constantly ask myself how in the world did I get blessed with so much love? My prayer for you is that you would know Jesus in a very real way. I have spent the majority of my life comprehending I am a son of God that is completely loved and whole through my faith in Jesus Christ.

I pray that you would have the assurance of The Fathers love. And that your hearts would be open to knowing Him in an intimate way. If you allow Him He will be there in your darkest hour, brightest day and for everything in between. Live by faith, one day at a time. I love you and "May the grace of the Lord Jesus Christ, the love of God, and the fellowship of the Holy Spirit be with you all (2 Corinthians 13:14)."

-Dad

PREFACE

Just Believe was written to inspire, invoke and ignite a culture of life-giving faith around the world. More than ever, in times like this, when the media, worldly systems, and modern culture attempts to discredit and damage the reputation of Jesus and His church, we need to be charged, and reminded why our faith in Jesus matters. I wrote this book for people who don't believe Jesus is the Christ our Messiah. I wrote this book for the individual who has gone through traumatic experiences and is constantly wondering how God could allow pain and suffering in their life. This book was also written for those who have been disappointed by people and or the church and have had their faith rocked to the core. It was also written for people who are struggling or in search of their true identity. My hope is that this book would encourage all who may be struggling in their faith; or looking for an opportunity to strengthen what already exists. Despite popular belief, the funny thing about faith is that God doesn't ask us to start off with a lot of it, but to allow space and opportunity for it to grow. My prayer is that this book, *Just Believe*, will take you on a journey that will lead to strengthening your belief in God. My desire is that everyone who reads or listens to this book will pray with the assurance of Nehemiah and that you wholeheartedly obey the will of the Lord for your life like Daniel. I also pray that your heart would be fulfilled serving the Lord and His people, like Martha and have the faith to believe like Mary. My hope is that you would study and dig deeper into the things of God like Paul, be empowered through faith to boldly build like Noah, and ultimately love like Jesus.

INTRODUCTION

Faith creates the space for God to do the unimaginable. When we choose to allow faith to govern our hearts and our lives, it gives God the space He needs to do His best work in us. Most of the time, when we deal with the effects of our own humanity we tend to not understand why we are doing some of the things we do. Have you ever done something that you said you would never do? Well, if you haven't, let me share with you some of my own personal experiences. I remember saying that I would never gain weight again after I lost 100 pounds. I vowed that I would never allow myself to get back to being a pleasantly plump individual, but after six years of blissful marriage and three chicken nugget loving and pizza obsessed children later, here I am back to the same size I was prior to losing the 100 pounds. I won't even mention how hard I worked initially to get the weight off in the first place. I also said that I would never drink coffee either. Yes, coffee. At one time in my life, I thought coffee was a legal drug that people used as a crutch to compensate for their own lack of discipline, yet here I am writing at this very moment with a French vanilla Iced Coffee with an added espresso shot, who would have thought?

What I'm trying to say is, often times we make decisions and do things in our lives because of the condition of our heart. Proverbs 4:23 tells us to guard our heart because out of it flows the issues of life. Let me let you in on a little secret, we do the things we do because of the condition of our human heart. The human heart is a complex system that governs so much of what we think and how we act. The crazy thing is that most of the time we are unaware of how it's affecting our daily lives. This makes clear that the human heart, which is governed by human nature, wars against the knowledge of God. Not only does our heart war against God, but it can be quite dark and evil.

Mark 7:21-23 says, "For it is from within, out of a person's heart, that evil thoughts come—sexual immorality, theft, murder, adultery, greed, malice, deceit, lewdness, envy, slander, arrogance, and folly. All these evils come from inside and defile a person."

The only way that we can prevent being deceived or falling prey to the evil desires of our heart, is to be born again (John 3:1-21). This happens when we invite the person of the Holy Spirit to come live within our hearts and we publicly, in word and deed, make Jesus the Lord over our lives. How can one be born again? It is through faith in Jesus

Christ! The Bible lets us know that faith, our ability to believe in God and obey Him, pleases God.

Hebrews 11:6 (The Living Bible) says, "You can never please God without faith, without depending on him. Anyone who wants to come to God must believe that there is a God and that He rewards those who sincerely look for him."

The late world-renowned evangelist Billy Graham wrote, "Faith pleases God more than anything else." The Christian life is dependent upon faith. We stand on faith; we live on faith. Faith is loved and honored by God more than any other single thing. The Bible teaches that faith is the only approach that we have to God. No man has sins forgiven, no man goes to heaven, and no man has assurance of peace and happiness until he has faith in Jesus Christ. In order to please God, you must believe in Him. Perhaps your faith is small and weak. It does not matter how big your faith is, but rather where your faith is.

After going through various types of life experiences, one of the greatest revelations of my life is knowing that God is with me. Though I have never physically seen Jesus, I know through faith that I have been healed by His love, empowered by His spirit and transformed by His Word. Our faith in God provides us with the authentic and unique opportunity to supernaturally encounter Jesus on a daily basis. Not only does faith give God the room He desires to be God in our lives, but it also opens our hearts to receive everything that God has for us.

When we choose to believe God it gives Him the freedom to turn our dilemmas or impossible situations into divine opportunities to experience His grace and goodness. Just like Jesus at the wedding party when the host ran out of wine, Jesus stepped into the middle of his dilemma and performed a miracle by turning water into wine. How about when Jesus was traveling to Jerusalem and met ten men who had been cast out of their families and communities because of the illnesses they had?

When they saw Jesus approaching, they screamed for His help and after seeing their situation Jesus completely healed them. What about the time Jesus fed thousands of people with two fish and five loaves of bread; or when He blessed Hannah, a woman that was barren, with a child; or when He raised Lazarus, a dead man, from the grave? Just as Jesus was able to step into all of these dilemmas, He's more than willing and able to step into yours.

I remember being in college and not having the money to pay my monthly tuition bill. I was a nervous wreck as I agonized about how I was going to be able to stay in school. For some, school was one of many options, but for me it was my only option. I knew it was the difference between going back to a life of poverty and brokenness, or setting myself up for a brighter future. Long story short, my degrees have been conferred upon, and I am able to provide a life for my children that I was not privileged to have. Even in being a father of three, and sometimes feeling I have the weight of the world on my shoulders, I am stopped by the Holy Spirit and reminded that Jesus is Jehovah Jireh, the Lord our Provider, and He is the master at stepping into what may seem like an impossible situation and creating a miracle.

I admonish you today, instead of focusing on the size of the problems in your life, look at them through faith, as opportunities for God to show up and perform unimaginable miracles. This is important because miracles reveal Jesus' magnificence and relevance in the earth. God wants to reveal the glory of His Son in us and through us (John 17:22). One of the ways He does this is through miracles, thus manifesting His glory in His Church (Isaiah 60:1-3). Miracles are physical, yet supernatural, expressions of God's love for His children. They confirm God's Word, point to the cross, and are the result of the completed work that Jesus did on the cross that provides opportunity for salvation, healing and deliverance for all people. Miracles result in people believing in Jesus. In Acts, people believed and joined the church by the thousands after miracles were performed.

Author Helen Calder said, "The signs that Jesus performs speak of the Father's mercy and love for people, as well as His dominion and power. They speak of His grace and generosity and His purposes."

Can Jesus use your life so that people can see and experience Him? Are you willing to allow your life to be a submitted tool for people to see Him and experience His heart and His Glory? Will you let your life be a sign and miracle for people who don't know Him? Better yet, when people see your life will they see Jesus?

The purpose of this book is to take you on a journey where your faith can be strengthened. Life has a way of hitting us so hard to the point that it attempts to knock our faith right out of us. As you read, ask yourself the hard questions and examine your heart. Allow the Holy Spirit to do surgery on the broken, wounded, hurting and infected parts of your life. My prayer is that you would experience the healing presence of God. May his love flood all of your being and fill you with new faith, hope and joy.

"Everything is possible for one who believes."

MARK 9:23

—JESUS

* * *

CHAPTER 1
FAITH IS EVERYTHING TO GOD

#Just Believe

"Those that come to God must first believe that He is and is a rewarder of them that diligently seek him." -Hebrews 11:6

As a little boy, I grew up believing that I could be anything. I believed I could be and do anything that my mind could conceive or imagine. At seven years old, I was asked that infamous question for the first time, "What do you want to be when you grow up?" Well, I vividly remember believing that I was going to be a famous speaker who would travel around the world. I also desired to be a doctor; no specific type of doctor, but one that walked around in a long white lab coat giving people shots in their arms. As a child, the world seemingly gave me permission to believe in whatever I could imagine. If I imagined and believed that the sky was green, that's what it was. Not only was that my reality, but all my friends would play along; allowing me to live out what I believed. My mom accepted every one of my imaginary friends. Those friends created imaginary worlds that dared me to dream and be whatever and do whatever supported the height, breath, and fluidity of my imagination running wild like an ocean with no boundaries and no waves to crash the ember that birthed the reality of it. There were no limitations or boundaries, just the assurance of what I believed.

I remember my parents and teachers would laugh and awe at my cute and probably very messy art projects that were guided and influenced by what I saw in my head and felt in my heart, but never actually saw with my eyes. Like my imagination, faith sort of works the same way. Hebrews 11:1 (NCV) says, "Faith is being sure of the things we hope for and knowing that something is real even if we do not see it." Pastor Eddie Leon of City Lights Church in Chicago, IL said it best, "Faith is choosing to take God at His word and obeying it."

Faith is the foundational building block of creation. It's choosing to bear witness to what you do not physically see, but know within your heart, mind, and soul is valid. To many, choosing to have faith in God seems crazy and outdated. People always ask me how do you believe in a God you don't see? My answer to that question is always, "I have never physically seen Him, but through faith I've experienced His love, joy, forgiveness, and splendor through His creation." Your ability to believe in God's Word means everything to Him.

Mark 13:31 reads, "Heaven and earth will pass away, but my words shall not pass away." "The word of the Lord abides forever." "The grass withers, the flower fades, but the word of our God stands forever."

These scriptures point out that everything in life may change over time or even change in a moment, but His Word will not. His truth never changes. There are no take backs. It is vital as Christians in a postmodern world to believe in God's Word because it creates a firm foundation for us to stand upon while we are amongst the different thoughts, theories, and philosophies about everything in the world. Our belief in God becomes a compass that we can use to navigate through the challenges, trials, and hard decisions we may have to make in everyday life.

Prayer: May my heart dare to believe again. May my mind be renewed by the truth of God's Word. May I undeniably know that Jesus is real and that He is madly in love with me. May every footprint of doubt and fear be permanently erased from my memory, and may I have the assurance that the Lord is with me and for me. In Jesus name, Amen.

CHAPTER 2
FAITH IS MORE THAN A FEELING

#Just Believe

"Therefore, preparing your minds for action, and being sober-minded, set your hope fully on the grace that will be brought to you at the revelation of Jesus Christ." -1 Peter 1:13

Many stories in the Bible highlight the life of people who had great faith.

Noah

God told Noah to build an ark because He was going to bring a massive flood. Noah took God at His word and built the ark.

Abraham

God told Abraham to go out to a place that he would receive as an inheritance. Abraham took God at His word, left everything he knew, and went to a foreign land.

Sarah

God told Sarah, an old woman, that she would conceive a son. Hebrews 11:11 states, "She considered Him faithful who had promised." She took God at His word.

Has your faith in God ever made you look crazy or foolish? I can think of many times when the Holy Spirit pushed me to do something like pray for someone in public, share my testimony with someone at work, or give the last little bit of money I had to someone on the street. If you're anything like me, these situations tend to leave you feeling super uncomfortable and completely taken out of a box of comfort. However, when we choose to shut down our emotions, when we are obedient to the prompting of the Holy Spirit, and we respond in faith, lives are forever changed!

Regardless of circumstances, logic, reason, or how we feel, like Noah, Abraham, and Sarah, we need to choose to believe God and obey Him. What would have happened if any of them were not obedient to what God instructed them to do and instead let their emotions get the best of them? In Noah's case, everyone, including him and his family, would have drowned. Abraham would have never received his promise, and Sarah would have continued to remain barren. Consequently, Jesus would never have entered the world, and there would be no reason for you to read this book. What I am trying to say is that sometimes faith will not make sense and it is in those moments that our emotions often get the best of us.

As a result, we never really experience all that God wants to do in us and through us because we allow our fears, anxiety, or lack of belief in God to hinder us from living our best lives. Smith Wigglesworth said it like this, *"There is nothing impossible with God. All the impossibility is with us when we measure God by the limitations of our unbelief."*

When we allow our feelings to cripple our faith, it does not just impact our lives, but it affects the lives of those who are supposed to see Jesus through us. *Have you ever allowed your emotions to cripple your faith? Have you ever ignored the prompting of the Holy Spirit when He asked you to do something you may have been uncomfortable with, or that seemed odd at the moment?* If so, next time think about how your decision to ignore Him will impact the lives of those around you who are supposed to see and experience Jesus through your faith.

In looking at the lives of so many people in the Bible, we learn that true faith in God pushes you to move and live in obedience to what He asks. As a believer, it's not enough to merely say, "I believe in God," which by the way has become very popular. We've all seen rappers, singers, actors and entertainers who have shown no regard for God get up when they win an award and the first thing out of their mouth is, " I thank God for..." when God had nothing to do with whatever they won their award for. I know that sounds a little judgmental and it is to an extent. If we don't judge what has been presented as "faith" in God by people who have influence; the definition and essence of what faith really is and how to govern your life by it will get lost and become watered down by people who don't know what it is.

According to the book of James, the Bible teaches us that, "Faith without action is pointless." Therefore, pleasing God happens when we have faith and apply it to action. Remember God is more concerned about our commitment to holiness not happiness.

The lives that we live at home, work, school, with family and/or with friends should be reflective of our belief in God. Our faith and obedience complement each other. Neither one promises convenience, but both yield much fruit. As believers in God, we have to be sure to put our feelings, intellect, and logic in check. Our faith is weakened when we filter it through our carnal flesh. One of the many reasons we have to put our feelings in check is because, for many of us, our emotions are typically governed by our heart. Despite popular opinion, the Bible in Jeremiah 17:9 describes the heart as being deceitful and desperately wicked. Most people live and are by-products of a 'feelings driven' culture. We do what we want, when we want, and how we want. We often live our lives on our own accord with very little regard for others or consequences. I've seen this take place with so many individuals, especially Christians. It's sad to see someone who was once on fire for God become lukewarm and then ice cold because of their inability to prioritize their feelings over their faith. I have seen some of the strongest Christians walk away from the Lord because they decided to make their faith in God bow to their feelings. When we do this, we literally make our feelings our "god". There is nothing wrong with listening to our feelings, they are God -given gifts, but when they are tainted by ungodly affections that live inside of our untrustworthy hearts and wrongly placed they can become idols. When I look on social media it is clear to see that we are a part of a time period where decisions are driven by emotions rather than God's word.

Can you believe it? The Bible calls the human heart untrustworthy! Though this may be a difficult pill to swallow, I'm sure we can all think of a time when our heart blinded us and led us to make decisions that we were not very proud of.

I have a simple question for you. *What happens when you don't feel like doing the right thing?*

There have been so many times that I have caught myself between a rock and a hard place because I just didn't feel like doing the right thing. Remember the time you were told not to touch the stove because it was hot, but you did it anyway? The truth of the matter is, much hasn't changed. Since the beginning of humanity, humans have been touching fires hoping not to get burned. If I can be honest, though I'm not very proud to admit it, there are many days that I just don't feel like doing the right thing or living up to the fullness of who God has called me to be. It's called being human. Being human means you will not be perfect and you will make mistakes. Being human and having faith in Jesus gives you the wisdom, power and tools you need to prevent making unnecessary mistakes and grants you the grace to recover when you do.

Crazy Relationship

In my early 20's, I was a mess. Due to my own brokenness and lack of accountability and love, I found myself in a toxic relationship that I personally knew would lead me down a path of headache and heartbreak. To this day, I look back and ask myself what in the world was I thinking? Clearly, I wasn't. I pursued this relationship, ignored the leading of the Holy Spirit, and the wisdom from people that loved me. I did all of this because it felt good to me at the moment. I admit I was intoxicated by feelings of lust, pride, and feeling wanted. It's amazing to me how we throw wisdom, reason, and sometimes Jesus away for something or someone who we know is no good for us. I call these things *painful pleasures* because they are high stake relationships that wind up costing us way more than what we bargained to pay. The crazy thing is that I almost married this individual listening to my feelings. I had to learn the hard way that everything that glistens isn't gold and everything that feels good isn't good. In that moment, I sold my faith to my feelings and in return contracted a sexually transmitted disease that thankfully penicillin could cure, but would forever stain my life. I had to learn the hard way that sin plays for keeps. Please don't make the same mistake I did, but let faith govern your heart and not your feelings. Remember, your emotions should not drive your life. They are God given, and we must allow them to be a gauge, not a guide.

Prayer:

May the Lord empower me with the strength and strategy to put my feelings in check and not to make decisions based off of emotions, but by the word of the Lord. In Jesus name, Amen.

CHAPTER 3
FAITH FUELS TRANSFORMATION

#JustBelieve

"And do not imitate this world, but be transformed by the renovation of your minds, and you shall distinguish what the good, acceptable and perfect will of God is." -Romans 12:2

Romans 12:2 is one of my favorite Bible scriptures. The first sermon I ever preached entitled, "It's Time for Change," is based from this very same text. I remember being as nervous as a pig in a slaughterhouse. My hands were sweating and my mother let me wear my step-father's tie and tie clip. The book of Romans depicts a people who are in transition from their traditionally immoral life to figuring out what it means to not just be a Christian, but to identify what it means to be a follower of Jesus.

Rev. Chuck Swindoll states, "Paul, in the book of Romans, showed how human beings lack God's righteousness because of our sin, receives God's righteousness when God justifies us by faith, demonstrates God's righteousness by being transformed from rebels to followers, confirms His righteousness when God saves the Jews, and applies His righteousness in practical ways throughout our lives."

The Roman church was filled with diverse people from various places. It was the epicenter of diversity. They housed everything from ruthless sailors and duteous traders to wealthy businessmen and the common enslaved Christians. Yes, Christians were slaves.

This prominent historic city like many of ours was overrun with different social issues and injustices. It was also known for being a solace for sexual immorality and idol worship. These people were absolute freaks! Their culture was driven by sexual promiscuity to the point where they turned into a type of worship that they gave to a demonic god. The Apostle Paul, their first pastor wrote a letter to them about their behavior and super sexually driven culture.

When he wrote to the Roman church he reminded them of the power of God's grace to miraculously and completely change lives. He used his own experience as a blueprint to physically demonstrate what God could do in a person's life. I don't know if you know Paul's story but at one point in his life he was a hitman who took pleasure in killing Christians. His letter was written to an unconventional community of people trying to figure out what it meant to embrace their new identity in Christ in an era where it was unpopular. It's super easy to be a Christian when your surrounded by Christians, but these individuals were surrounded by a culture that had no limits or boundaries on what was acceptable behavior. Anything went!

I think most modern believers forget or don't realize that to be a follower of Jesus during Bible times was almost the same as being labeled a religious zealot.

Yet, in the face of this, early believers rejected the religious and ceremonial beliefs of the Pharisees and Sadducees and clung to the gospel, the good news of Jesus Christ. They left what was familiar to them to embrace their future hope in Christ Jesus who had become the author and finisher of their faith. We can learn a thing or two from the Roman church. We learn that transformation is an acquired taste that is not for the faint of heart; and that change begins when we are willing to abandon who we think we are for who He says we can be. In order for this to happen, the process of transformation, will often times destroy our box and comfort zones that we called home or normal. It's hard, but when you understand God loves you, you'll trust his process even when you disagree or are uncomfortable.

One of my favorite teachers, Richard G. Scott states, "A consistent, righteous life produces an inner power and strength that can be permanently resistant to the eroding influence of sin and transgression." In other words, your faith and character are closely related. The more your faith influences your daily actions, despite how you may personally think or feel about them at that moment, a Christ-like character is slowly being formed in you. This Christ-like character creates a lens for you to see your life and the world as Christ does. The Bible teaches us that there is always a war between our flesh and our spirit. Simply put, the part of us that is flesh, or prone to sin, wars against God and our spirit man.

Both flesh and spirit have an appetite, and every day you have to decide which one you are going to feed. I'm sure you've seen a movie, or a cartoon that displays this as an angel and a devil sitting on either side of a person's shoulder trying to influence the individual's decision making. In most cases, the person chooses to listen to the devil or their flesh consciousness, which tends to lead them down a path full of uncertainty and unnecessary mistakes. It is when we decide to practice listening to the Holy Spirit or our God consciousness that we are transformed. The question is why is it essential to make it a way of life to listen to the Holy Spirit (God consciousness) and how do I practically do that?

Watch How You Live Your Life

Faith and obedience to God's Word creates a supernatural strength. Faith and obedience produce a God-like character and as a result opens the door to the supernatural. This is the ethos of God's heart that creates the fuel needed to make necessary changes in one's life.

Your daily exercise of faith in every little and big decision you make strengthens and builds upon this strength; which increases your character and expands your capacity to say no to temptation and sin. This God-like character is developed daily and is made to be used in moments of great temptation and hardship. As a result, your capacity and confidence to conquer the trials and temptations in your life are supernaturally enhanced. The more your character is built, the more empowered you are to benefit from exercising the power of faith.

"Character is woven patiently from threads of applied principle, doctrine, and obedience." - Richard G Scott

The thing about getting where we believe God has called or chosen us to be, may feel like it's taking forever. Maybe you're like me and don't necessarily deny God's ability to bring change in someone's life, but sometimes doubt His willingness to do it in your own personal experience. Know that being a disciple of Jesus does not mean that He expects us to come to Him as perfect beings. God tends to call unqualified, dirty, broken, and hurting people and He qualifies, cleans, repairs, and heals them. It's not in our ability, but in our availability, that makes us candidates for a wonderful transformation. If you still think that you are beyond God's reach, look at some of the people that God called and who they were before being transformed. [1]

Noah was a drunk. (Genesis 9:21)
Abraham was too old. (Genesis 17:17)
Isaac was a liar, just like his Dad. (Genesis 26:7, 20:2)
Jacob was a liar & a schemer. (Genesis 27:19)
Leah was unattractive. (Genesis 29:17)
Joseph was abused. (Genesis 37:18f and many more!)
Moses had a speech problem. (Exodus 4:10)
Gideon was afraid. (Judges 6:27)
Samson had long hair and was a womanizer. (Judges 16:17,14:2,16:1)
Rahab was a prostitute. (Joshua 2:1, 6:17)
Jeremiah and Timothy were too young.. (Jeremiah 1:6, 1 Timothy 4:12)
David was an adulterer and a murderer. (2 Samuel 12:9)
Elijah was suicidal. (1 Kings 19:4)
Isaiah preached naked. (Isaiah 20:2-3)
Jonah ran from God. (Jonah 1:3)
Naomi was a bitter widow. (Ruth 1:20)
Job went bankrupt. (Job 1:13-19)
Peter denied Christ. (Matthew 26:69-74)
The Disciples fell asleep while praying. (Matthew 26:40-43)
Martha worried about everything. (Luke 10:40-41)
The Samaritan woman was divorced, more than once. (John 4:18)
Zacchaeus was too small. (Luke 19:3)
Paul was too religious. (Philippians 3:4-6)
Timothy had an ulcer. (1 Timothy 5:23)
Lazarus was dead. (John 11:1-44)

Trust God with your transformation. Remember, we are His masterpiece. He has created us anew in Christ Jesus so we can do the right things he planned for us long ago (Ephesians 2:10)." No one, including you, is perfect, but we are God's artwork continuously being perfected. I don't know about you, but that takes so much pressure off of me to appear like I have it all together. It permits me to stand in the truth of my own brokenness and know that all of the broken pieces of my life will be used to the glory of God to make something beautiful. The beauty of being called a masterpiece is that before the artwork is completed, it goes through various stages that may look a hot mess to people who do not have creative control of the project. But, you can count on the artist knowing how the mess will eventually come together and what purpose it will serve when it is completed.

Prayer: "Have mercy on me, O God, because of your loyal love! Because of your great compassion, wipe away my rebellious acts! Wash away my wrongdoing! Cleanse me of my sin! For I am aware of my rebellious acts; I am forever conscious of my sin. Against you – you above all – I have sinned; I have done what is evil in your sight. So you are just when you confront me; you are right when you condemn me. Look, I was guilty of sin from birth, a sinner the moment my mother conceived me. Look, you desire integrity in the inner man; you want me to possess wisdom. Sprinkle me with water, and I will be pure; wash me, and I will be whiter than snow. Grant me the ultimate joy of being forgiven! May the bones you crushed rejoice! Hide your face from my sins! Wipe away all my guilt! Create for me a pure heart, O God! Renew a resolute spirit within me! Do not reject me! Do not take your Holy Spirit away from me! Let me again experience the joy of your deliverance! Sustain me by giving me the desire to obey! Then I will teach rebels your merciful ways, and sinners will turn to you. Rescue me from the guilt of murder, O God, the God who delivers me! Then my tongue will shout for joy because of your deliverance. O Lord, give me the words! Then my mouth will praise you." - Psalm 51:1-15

CHAPTER 4
FAITH+HOPE = PERSEVERANCE

#JustBelieve

"Consider it pure joy, my brothers and sisters, whenever you face trials of many kinds because you know that the testing of your faith produces perseverance. Let perseverance finish its work so that you may be mature and complete, not lacking anything." - *James 1:3-4*

Life happens. We can all identify with this short, yet powerful statement. Plans get changed, and our goals get altered. Sometimes, the turbulence of life rocks us to our core. One of the hardest things to do is to continue to live when you no longer see the point of doing so anymore. It's sad to say, but sometimes life throws blows that knock the wind out of us while we are simultaneously trying to inhale and exhale the expectations of others around us. We are then forced to smile when we want to cry or cuss and sometimes do both.

The Apostles James and Paul taught us through scripture that trials produce perseverance, and perseverance produces character, and character hope (Romans 5:3-4). Perseverance is one's inner ability and determination to pursue something or achieve a goal despite its level of difficulty or delayed success. Have you ever wanted something that you felt was out of your reach? I have. We have. My wife and I always wanted to have multiple children, but early on in our marriage we experienced multiple miscarriages. A miscarriage is when an embryo or fetus dies prematurely which normally happens in the first trimester (3 months) of a pregnancy. Miscarriages can happen for a number of reasons, but it is never caused by something the pregnant woman did. My wife, Jackie wrote an amazing blog about our experience with miscarriage and I would like to share it with you.

Our Story:

The date was August 13th, 2014. I woke up, pregnant, at 6 A.M. I was excited for the ultrasound that was scheduled to take place at 10am that morning and I thanked God for answering my prayers.

I wondered whether the baby was a boy or a girl and dreamt about what my child would look like at his or her birth in March.

When I left the ultrasound, the clock read 11:30 A.M. And my baby was gone.

I was 8 weeks along when my husband, my mother, and I saw the ultrasound tech's face tense up. I read the news in her body language before I could comprehend the silence that reverberated throughout the room in the absence of a heartbeat. The sadness met me as I laid there attempting to read the tech's face of confusion as she couldn't find the baby in the sac. My heart broke for the loss of someone I never knew.

The ultrasound tech said she couldn't read the ultrasound and that I would need to wait until my OB nurse called me to read me the results. 4 hours passed and I never received a call. An hour after that the doctor herself called me to inform me that the baby stopped growing at 7 weeks and there was no longer a heartbeat.

I sat on the couch for hours and stared at nothing.

When I walked into my room, a dozen reminders of my
loss assaulted me – a baby blue piggy bank on our dresser that
my husband and I began to fill up for our future baby, a
box of diapers stored in the corner of our bedroom, and all
the baby books that the doctor had given me to read.

I touched the piggy bank and thought of the name we had
already picked out for the baby if it was a boy, Judah
Mateo Marshall. Tears lodged in my throat as I dropped to
my knees and cried there hysterically.

For a long time, I kneeled there crying until I couldn't stand
being in my bedroom anymore; so I moved into the living
room where our bookshelf holds all of our bibles and
encouraging books. In that moment, a scripture came to my
mind. It wasn't the scripture I would have expected. Not
a scripture of comfort, or hope in God's power, or a promise
of future blessings. It was one spoken by Job, when he was
faced with tragedy: "The Lord gave and the Lord has taken
away; may the name of the Lord be praised." Job 1:21 (NIV).

It was then that the tears came, a flood of them
came uncontrollably and I laid there shaking until my

husband walked in and held me until I calmed down. I knew about how God gave us a baby, and I was experiencing the agony of taking the child away, but how could I praise Him in the midst of a nightmare-come-true?

I was so upset with God that He would reveal to my husband that we were pregnant weeks before we actually knew and that God told him that it was a boy and that his name would be Judah. I was hurt that God would allow me to experience this type of hurt.

Days passed and every night as I laid in my bed to go to sleep, I was reminded of the nights my husband knelt down on the side of the bed and talked to the baby that didn't even have ears yet. I was reminded of the nights he prayed over me and the baby and proclaimed that the baby would grow full term. I was reminded of how willing and excited we were to change our entire lives for a child that wasn't even born yet; and how all of a sudden that all stopped. I cried myself to sleep for nights in a row and questioned, why me?

On Friday, August 15th I began to bleed. I knew it was coming, but when it did, it was a lot harder than what I thought it would be. I woke up Sunday night from my sleep at 12am

with extremely bad pain that wouldn't allow me to sleep.
After 2 showers and 5 hours of pain, the sac finally passed
Monday at 5am. I laid on the floor of my bedroom
crying and reminding myself that God was almighty and
that He was ultimately the giver of all things.

Tonight, I opened my bible and a bunch of pictures fell
out of different pages. In the book of 1 Samuel, this picture
laid as the bookmark.

My mother, pregnant with me in her belly.

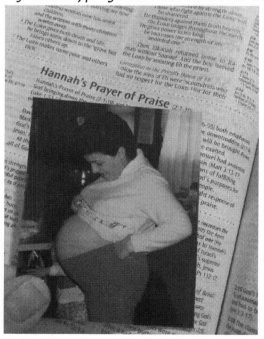

In 1 Samuel 2:6-8
it says, "The Lord gives
both death and life; he
brings some down to the
grave, but raises others
up. The Lord makes some
poor and others rich; he
brings some down and
lifts others up.

*He lifts the poor from the dust and the needy from
the garbage dump. He sets them among princes, placing
them in seats of honor. For all the earth is the Lord's, and
He has set the world in order."*

*I realized in that moment that suffering and sorrow are
not the enemies I'd once thought, but are tools in the
hands of a loving God to mold me into the woman
He desires me to be. I only need to keep seeking
Him, pouring my pain and doubts before Him, and
praising Him even when it's the last thing my flesh
wants to do.*

*Though I am still grieving the loss of our baby, I know
that God used that unborn child for a purpose in
His Kingdom and in my life. I will never be the same.
I know now, that my faith can no longer be based on
the ever-changing circumstances of my life but on
the unchanging glory and wonder of God. And
now, through the window of my suffering, I can see
God more clearly and I know that all things,
even miscarriage, can be transformed in His hands.*

How you go through trials and tribulations matter. Faith in Jesus sometimes doesn't fix our problems, but gives one the strength needed to walk through them. Faith in God in the midst of hellish situations provides a peace that makes no sense. This faith produces hope that gives anyone who believes the strength to persevere and that perseverance is fueled by a joyful expectation that cannot be faked or mass manufactured. This gift comes from God himself and it does not place us in denial, but it roots our hearts and emotions in the truth that we serve a good God who is in love with us and would never harm us. This God rather, has a great plan and future for our lives.

Perseverance is what is produced when we choose not to give up in the middle of the trial. This is the acknowledgment of our pain and our future hope that is in Christ Jesus. The Bible points out the importance of being steadfast and unwavering and preserve in trials which means to "bear up a heavy weight." When we do this, the fruits of the spirit are developed in us and makes us more Christ-like. This is the ultimate completed work of perseverance. After many tears, conversations, and counseling we have three amazing children who we thank

God for daily. Where you are is not the end of your story. Allow God to perform a miracle through your faith.

By now you've read a few things about Faith and how it should be the central point of every believer's life. The entire Christian Faith is based on the foundational belief that Jesus was born of a virgin named Mary. Mary, a woman that had never been touched by a man, divinely ends up pregnant with Jesus, our Lord and Savior. This Jesus, who walked the face of the earth as completely God and completely man at the same time, was known for healing the sick and raising the dead. He was beaten, and chose to hang on a cross for the redemption and restoration of you and me. This same Jesus challenged systems of injustice so that the least of these would know that they were loved and not forgotten. *Do you ever ask why He did all of this?* It's because He came to liberate those who were lost. And not only did He come to do this, but He also came to restore hope. Faith is the translator of God's heart, and it speaks from a prepared place. Trust that is put into action produces something that is called hope. This type of hope is fueled by a foundational belief in the goodness of God, which creates a "confident expectation" that God is sovereign and has our best interest at heart.

There are numerous examples in the Bible that point to the fact that God loves you and he has your best interest at heart. Here are a couple of my favorite:

Jeremiah 29:11 (The Message Bible)
I know what I'm doing. I have it all planned out—plans to take care of you, not abandon you, plans to give you the future you hope for.

Matthew 6:26-34 (New Living Translation)
Look at the birds! They don't worry about what to eat—they don't need to sow or reap or store up food—for your heavenly Father feeds them. And you are far more valuable to him than they are. Will all your worries add a single moment to your life? And why worry about your clothes? Look at the field lilies! They don't worry about theirs. Yet King Solomon in all his glory was not clothed as beautifully as they. And if God cares so wonderfully for flowers that are here today and gone tomorrow, won't he more surely care for you?

You see, it's quite simple, God is for you and His will for your life is good. This is sometimes challenging to believe for people who have gone through hard and trying times in their life because we genuinely ask questions like, "Why does God allow bad things to happen to good people? How does a good and loving God allow suffering? Why did God let my family member die? Or why didn't God stop a tragedy from happening?"

In all honesty, these are valid questions to ask because our faith is what fuels our hope or confident expectation that God is good and He loves us. The truth is I don't have the answers to these questions, but what my faith mixed with hope produces is perseverance. Perseverance is the supernatural ability to handle obstacles in the midst of hard and trying times. It is a resilient posture that urges you to plant your feet in the soil of faith so that you can be watered by streams of hope, believing that the goodness of God will produce the miraculous.

Prayer: May my faith in God produce a hope that enables me to persevere beyond all of life's obstacles and situations. As

I go about my day, may I have the assurance to know that God is with me and for me. In Jesus name, Amen.

CHAPTER 5
FAITH GIVES YOU THE STRENGTH TO FORGIVE

#JustBelieve

"Forgiveness isn't weakness, it's the ultimate sign of courage and strength." –Marie Forleo.

I don't know how I'm going to get through this chapter without tears streaming down my face. It has taken me a long time to understand that I can't forgive people in my own strength, because I have tried and it just does not work. I believe that the tears that I've cried are seeds that will produce a harvest of joy according to Psalm 126:5. I've decided to forgive my molesters who are still walking around today like it never happened. I've made attempts to forgive the pastors who called me "son", yet confessed my most in-depth, darkest and shameful life experiences. I've tried to forgive my mother for lying and concealing the identity of my father until she was cornered to tell the truth on my 25th birthday. I've even tried to forgive my biological father for not wanting to be in my life and to this day looks at me as his biggest mistake. I have tried to forgive people who I have helped, but they walked away, labeling me as their enemy for reasons I still don't know. Bottom line is, I need Jesus.

The Apostle Paul wrote to the early church while he was wrongly imprisoned for spreading the gospel of Jesus in 2 Corinthians 12:9–10, "My grace is sufficient for you, for my power is made perfect in weakness. Therefore I will boast all the more gladly about my weaknesses, so that Christ's power may rest on me. That is why, for Christ's sake, I delight in weaknesses, in insults, in hardships, in persecutions, in difficulties. For when I am weak, then I am strong."

What a powerful passage. What I get out of his words is that it's okay not to be okay. I understand that in this life hardships are going to try to dismantle and break you; and when they do that, we don't have to make attempts at being strong. We can collapse in the arms of Jesus, our heavenly

Father, and know that not only will we be safe, but when we can no longer fight or advocate for ourselves, Christ's power will rest on us for His sake. When calamity, heartbreak, drama, lies, accusations, false reports, and broken perceptions happen, and death seems more bearable than life, it is in those moments that our weakness positions us to receive the strength of our loving father.

The question that I often ask is, *"What do you do with the power He gives?"*

Since I'm being honest, there have been so many times that I have wanted to get even, lash out and gain revenge for some of the most painful situations that I've walked through. But I'm determined by the end of this chapter to allow the Holy Spirit to do deep surgery within my heart to cut away every bit of bitterness, anxiety, depression, doubt, self-hatred and anything else that has kept or is keeping me in any type of bondage. I'm genuinely going to believe everything that I say to you. I don't want to write this chapter and make you think that I'm an "expert" on forgiveness, but like you, by faith, I am working through the punches that life has thrown at me. My prayer is that we will all find the strength to forgive people that have caused offense in our lives, just as Jesus did when He hung on the cross and said, "Father, forgive them for they know not what they do."

"A bloody and unrecognizable Jesus looked down from the cross upon a scene that must have been distressing to Him. The Roman soldiers were gambling for His clothing; the criminals on the crosses to either side of Him were reviling Him; the religious leaders were mocking Him, and the crowd was blaspheming Him. Surrounded by this most unworthy people, Jesus prayed for them. "Father, forgive them" a prayer of unmatched mercy and love."[2]

Though I am growing in my faith in God daily, I have not "arrived" yet. Did I just say that? Yes, I'm not there yet. Pray for me. At times, I think about specific events in my life and ask, "Why me?" Have you ever asked yourself that question? From time to time, my life events play through my mind like a DVD that has been scraped on the asphalt of my heart and all I can think is, why me? Thus, causing more damage that never allows me to get through one entire scene without reliving the moment that plays over and over and over again. Those moments make me remember the smell of his cologne and the red Ford stick shift truck that taught me my first sex education lesson. It forces me to remember the sense of belonging that I felt when I was brought in front of the church and prophesied over and called "son" and was told I'd found my tribe, then quickly reminded that I'd been cast out like the weakest link on a Survivor episode, and never welcomed or restored back into the family. Let's not forget about the pain I feel every time I look at my children and they enthusiastically yell, "Daddy, Daddy, Daddy" or when they hurt themselves and my name is the first name they call to pick them up to acknowledge the pain that their "boo boo" is causing and they look to me to kiss it and say "It's going to be alright."

I know now that I will never experience that sense of security, love, acknowledgment, and affirmation from the man whose DNA shaped my very existence. I need Jesus. I can finally breathe and say like Joseph after being betrayed by his brothers, "Even though you intended to destroy me, God intended it only for my good, He kept me through it all so that countless people's lives would be saved."

Joseph's Story: He was the favorite of his father, Jacob. He had the coat of many colors, which his father made for him.

His brothers hated him so much because of his jacket and the dream God had given him as a young man, that they put him in a ditch, only to later sell him into slavery and lie to their father that a wild animal had killed him. In bondage, he served in Potiphar's house and from Potiphar's house, he went to prison for pleasing God (He said no to adultery). In prison he interpreted dreams for someone who later forgot about him. Some years later and something switched for Joseph. He went from jail to dominion, and now, he was second in command to Pharaoh.

During this period his brothers came to him for help, not recognizing him until Joseph made himself known. So now, Joseph brought his family to Egypt and gave them the best place in the land. Every day he sees the people that did him wrong and wanted him dead, yet he still greets them with joy. He totally forgives them by taking some necessary steps to receive his healing and breakthrough, which I believe can be helpful to all of our healing processes.

Joseph put the situation in perspective. In his statement, "You tried to destroy me, but God in His sovereignty took your evil and changed it for my good to save others' lives." We learn that though it is never okay for people to cause us pain or have evil intentions towards us, God doesn't allow our experience with pain or the trauma of it to go to waste. The thing is, most of us never get to that part of our process where we allow God to recycle what we've been through because we either spend the majority of our lives running from it or allowing it to cripple us to the point where we develop a victim mentality and never move forward and experience victory in Jesus.

I believe Joseph understood that his brother's broken understanding of his dream and their lack of love and support for him, which caused them to react in a rash and cruel way. Though I don't believe we should ever belittle or excuse people from their actions, I do believe there is some level of liberation when you humanize the person who may have caused the primary offense. We have to recognize that the person who caused the offense is broken and flawed and in need of the same love, grace, and mercy of God as you are.

The Christian faith is based on the foundational belief that we have been forgiven. Despite what we've done or where we've been, through the redemptive blood of Jesus Christ we are forgiven. This is not half-hearted forgiveness. The Bible talks about how once we come to God and ask for forgiveness, that He places our sins and transgressions into the sea of forgetfulness that is as far as the east is from the west. When you realize as a believer, that Christ has done that for you, how much more as children of God can we be like our heavenly Father and forgive those who have hurt or committed sin against us? This isn't an easy pill to swallow. We sometimes hold on to the person and the pain of the offense because it was unwarranted and underserved and the person(s) were guilty.

T.D. Jakes said it like this, "Forgiveness is a big idea, and for big people who are willing to grasp this concept that people who are innocent don't ask for forgiveness they ask for justice. People who are guilty often are in need of mercy, grace, and forgiveness."

The truth is, Joseph had every right to be angry, hurt, and seek revenge on his brothers. The bigger question is, what would he have accomplished by seeking revenge? If he had retaliated against his brothers, what good would it have done? If he'd gotten even, he may have had a moment of fulfillment seeing his brothers suffer, but it would not have changed his experience and the trauma he still had to live through? Freedom fighter Nelson Mandela wrote, "Resentment is like drinking poison and then hoping it will kill your enemies." Resenting the people that hurt or betrayed you doesn't do anything for you except keep you in a self-made prison. Like Joseph, look at your offenders through the eyes of Jesus and see them as innately broken and hurting individuals who are in need of the grace, love, and mercy of God.

I believe Joseph's brothers put him in a pit and sold him into slavery because they were weak and their weakness, lack of love, affection, and affirmation from their father drove them to make a weak decision. To help you put your experiences in perspective, I encourage you to write a letter of forgiveness. Yes, a letter of forgiveness. Think about the person(s) from your past that you are holding a grudge against or you haven't forgiven for whatever reason. When you write this letter, don't hold back. Please do yourself a favor and tell the truth. Now I have to warn you, this is not going to be an easy task because you will probably have to relive painful moments. The key is not to run away from the pain, but to process as you write. Grab a box of tissues, put some music on, and write down all that you need to say. Here is an example of an open letter I wrote to my father.

Dear Dad,

Yes, I am ok, as if you've ever asked.

I want to say happy Father's Day to the man that gave me his DNA. You have never and will never know the blessing of having me as a son. By virtue of your actions, I know that I have been blessed not to have you in my life. I've accepted the fact that God protected me from the toxicity of any relationship that would make me feel like I was not loved and wanted. I want to let you know today that God has and is setting me free from the pain and rejection that caused me to make so many stupid decisions in my life. I just want you to know that God has taken care of me all of my life and has sent special men, full of the Holy Ghost, to love me and show me who I am and who I will become. God has never missed a football game, prom, graduation or my wedding. I just wanted you to know that I am loved and have an amazing wife and 3 amazing children who adore me. I graduated from high school, college, and graduate school while working full time jobs to support me and my family. I have an amazing career giving young men and women the love and validation that you were never strong or whole enough to give me. I don't hate you anymore. I would be lying if I said I wasn't still a little upset. For a long time I couldn't understand why you would choose not to be in my life. I questioned why I wasn't good enough or smart enough to be accepted as your son. What could I do to earn your love, acceptance, affirmation and affection? Not until now have I realized that you not being in my life had nothing to do with me. It was all about you. I don't know who or what broke you, but I am praying for your healing and contending for your deliverance. I pray that you would experience the depth and intensity of God's love.

I've learned it's a love I don't have to work for
A love I don't have to do tricks for
A love I don't have to people please for
A love I could never earn
A love that I am still learning how to receive, but it's a love that brings me so much life and joy. Johnnie, I love you and happy Father's Day.

The Son You Would Be Blessed to Have,
Robert Marshall Jr.

The amazing thing about this assignment is that you don't send the letter. This exercise is for your personal healing, not an attempt to reconcile.

According to Psychologist Dr. J. Burke, "Forgiveness is not condoning the perpetrator's behavior, justifying their offense or excusing their behavior due to extenuating circumstances that made them act in that manner. It is not forgetting what happened to us or denying the harmful impact that perpetrator's behavior had on our lives. The act of forgiveness is also very different to reconciliation and does not imply rebuilding a relationship with the perpetrator. Instead, forgiveness is the healing of ourselves by replacing negative feelings, thoughts, and behaviors associated with the perpetrator and their act with their real equivalent.

For example, when we forgive someone, we replace the thoughts of revenge with goodwill or at least acceptance of the offender. For example, when your former partner leaves you for someone else, you may spend weeks, months, years ruminating about it, bad-mouthing him or her, and seeking revenge on them. This way, every time you think of them, see their picture or bump into them, you will experience a lot of negative emotions, which will make you feel bad. However, when you forgive, your life will improve for the better. Every time you think of them, they will no longer make you feel bad; instead, you will feel positive and accepting." [3]

Joseph recognized God's goodness and purpose in his pain. God, like a good farmer, doesn't throw away the manure in our lives, but uses it to assure our growth through all seasons of life. Let's not forget Joseph's entire experience stemmed from a dream that God gave him, not one he asked for.

According to Genesis 37:5-11, "Joseph had a dream, and when he told it to his brothers, they hated him all the more. He said to them, "Listen to this dream I had: We were binding sheaves of grain out in the field when suddenly my sheaf rose and stood upright, while your sheaves gathered around mine and bowed down to it." His brothers said to him, "Do you intend to reign over us? Will you actually rule us?" And they hated him all the more because of his dream and what he had said. Then he had another dream, and he told it to his brothers. "Listen," he said, "I had another dream, and this time the sun and moon and eleven stars were bowing down to me." When he told his father as well as his brothers, his father rebuked him and said, "What is this dream you had? Will your mother and I and your brothers actually come and bow down to the ground before you?" His brothers were jealous of him, but his father kept the matter in mind."

Joseph's brother's hatred for him had nothing to do with what he had done to them. The favoritism he received from his father bothered them, but the dream He received from God is what caused them to hate and get rid of him. You would think sharing his God-given dream with his family would have caused them to celebrate what God wanted to do in their lives, but due to their own broken understanding and a weak interpretation of this dream, they tried to get rid of Joseph instead of nurturing him. Joseph's vision did not create a cushion for him, but instead, it opened up the doors of hell and hardship from the moment he opened his mouth. As we look at his journey from the pit to the palace, we see God's goodness and unraveling purpose for Joseph being discovered through each stage of his journey.

We are not always going to understand what God is doing in our lives. Our faith should make us alright with this fact. Joseph's dream caused him to lose his coat, get put in a ditch, sold into slavery, and falsely accused by a married woman that wanted to have sexual intercourse with him. It led to him being thrown into a dungeon, where he was forgotten about even after helping someone else get out of jail. Through everything he went through, we see God's goodness and faithfulness in the midst of the pain and calamity he was going through in his life. The mere fact that Joseph lives to tell his own story is a testament to God's faithfulness. Ultimately Joseph finds himself the second in command to Egypt and has the most significant opportunity to help people who need it the most, including his family. Remember, God can turn your trash into treasure while turning your misery into ministry, if you let him.

He forgave them. #Selah. Lastly, Joseph said, "I am not God, I release you."Let's be honest, it's time to let the people go who hurt you. Nelson Mandela said, "Un-forgiveness is like drinking poison waiting or someone else to die. Un-forgiveness makes you a prisoner of your own thoughts. It locks you in a cell with the person(s) who caused you the pain you're battling with now. This prevents you from experiencing any true breakthrough, happiness, or growth because your energy is spent replaying what they did to you over and over again. If you're like me, for a long time I couldn't listen to certain songs or visit certain places because it reminded me of a specific person or a traumatic event.

If you are experiencing any of what I previously talked about, you are more than likely harboring un-forgiveness in your heart and are in a unhealthy cycle that causes you to relive the offense(s) that have taken place in your life. Did you know every time you do this to yourself you become a victim all over again? For real, it's like it happened all over again. When you choose to hold on to grudges or un-forgiveness, you form demonic and toxic spiritual bonds call soul-ties. Did you know you can be bound together through unhealthy emotional soul-ties, or bitter root judgments or vows when using words like "I will never forgive them for what they did to me?" We often use binding words like this when we have placed our confidence and trust in someone who has exploited and betrayed us. Bitterness, resentment, and bitter root judgments bind us to the person that hurt or offended us." [4]

This type of betrayal can occur within our families, jobs, friendships, and or in intimate relationships, but as you may know this often times happens within the four walls of the Church. It is imperative for us to choose, as an act of our will, to forgive our betrayers. Releasing the offense and our offender to God through faith releases us and allows God to undertake justice on our behalf. God has given us free will to choose our response, and He will not violate or override our will even if it might be in our best interest.

The Bible teaches in Romans 12:19-2, "Beloved, never avenge yourselves, but leave it to the wrath of God, for it is written, "Vengeance is mine, I will repay, says the Lord."

Our unwillingness to forgive someone allows fear to grip our heart and soul, and build what is called a fortress or a stronghold that prevents us from being hurt again. Did you know that un-forgiveness also prevents God from responding to your prayers? When iniquity is formed in our hearts, it blocks God from hearing us.

Many times we are like the man whose debt was forgiven entirely but then hastened someone else who owed him money. Ask yourself who you have been holding hostage within you. Who have you bound? Who keeps you in a mode of consistent discontent? Do yourself a huge favor. Find a quiet area, lift your hands and at this moment close your eyes and go back to the place where the offense took place. Tell the person that offended you, "I forgive you." Let the tears flow, live in the moment and let them go. Choose to receive your healing and breakthrough. Like Joseph, instead of punishing his offenders for what they did to him, he let them know that their weak decision to try to get rid of him was a part of God's plan to put him in the palace. Through faith, God will make something unusual out of the broken pieces of your life.

When I get overwhelmed by the things that have happened in my life, I remember a saying that my mother taught me. She would always look at me and say, "Son, God makes all things beautiful in His time." It is hard to believe that when the pain of your past is weighing on your shoulders and you're battling through feelings of fear, anxiety, and depression. You have three options when you go through hardships, you can either let it define you, let it destroy you or allow it to strengthen you. Remember, our scars remind us of where we've been, but they don't have to define where we are going.

Prayer: Below is a beautiful prayer that was written by Hope for the Broken Hearted Ministries. I encourage you to become familiar with it. God knows it's helped me.

"Dear Heavenly Father,

I come to you and ask for your help. I know that I am to forgive others as you have forgiven me, but I find it so hard to do Lord. My mind and heart are full of anger for the things that have been said and done. At times it seems as though the ones that inflict pain and wounds are unrepentant...that they escape judgment. I am angry for what they have taken from me and for the pain they have caused me.

Lord, please help me to see with your eyes. Help me to remember that forgiveness is for me and not for them. Help me to remember that my forgiveness does not depend on them apologizing or repenting...help me to remember that forgiveness is between you and me. Lord, I am releasing my pain, and my hurt and my anger to you and I am asking for your help in forgiving them so I can be set free.

I want to forgive and leave this heavyweight at your feet so I can be set free. Lord, their sin and their wrongdoing, I leave in your hands for You to deal with it. I no longer want to be held hostage in a prison of anger, bitterness and sadness for what has been done by someone else. I no longer want to serve the sentence for what someone else has done wrong.

Lord, release me from this bondage and free my heart. I want to forgive Lord, as you have forgiven me. You died not only to set me free from my sins, but to set me free from all the things that hold me hostage and keep me from being who you want me to be. Help me to live in the peace and freedom that you offer.

Lord, from this day forward, I want to be healed from all these negative feelings. Thank you Lord, for helping me. What I can't do and what I don't have the strength to do in my own power, I know I am able to do through Jesus.

Thank you Lord for helping me to move forward today. Help me turn to you when old feelings and thoughts start to enter my mind. Bind the enemy so he can't bring up the past. Clean the wound out of my heart Lord so it can finally heal and so it can be at peace. Thank you, Lord. In the name of Jesus, I ask all of these things, Amen.

CHAPTER 6
FAITH OPENS DOORS TO MIRACLES

#JustBelieve

"Every day holds the possibility of a Miracle" - Job 5:9

With each step, it is our faith in God that gives us the assurance that our steps are being ordered by the Lord. When we misstep or make mistakes, often times it is a result of us allowing our reasoning, fear, or flat out disbelief to cloud our decision-making. The beautiful thing about the grace and mercy of God is that our faith in knowing that Jesus loves and will forgive us can help us to continue on our path to glory. That glorious path, known as miracles, cannot be obtained without faith. Faith is putting trust in Jesus and allowing Him to help you step gracefully back on your path. Faith is that confidence you have to achieve something in your life. Faith is the reassurance you get that you can and will climb over that mountain no matter how difficult. Without faith one is lost on that path. How does one open the door to miracles without faith? It's impossible.

Faith is the environment in which miracles take place. Without trials, hardships or needs, we have no need for miracles in our lives. I think most folks forget that miracles require a certain type of environment if we look at the miracles of Jesus you will find a trend that every person that was in need and received a healing or some type of deliverance where at their worst. From turning water into wine to healing people from leprosy we learn that miracles often times are manifested when people are at a breaking point. Jesus tends to have the tendency to wait until folks are sometimes dead to perform miracles (Ask Lazarus).

Smith Wigglesworth, a healing evangelist, taught, "Great faith only comes through great trials."

It is necessary to experience the tension of pain and trial to see the work of God in the world. The Apostle Paul encouraged early church believers by telling them that whatever we are facing in our lives at the moment are not worthy to be compared to the Glory that will be revealed in us. Your impossible situation produces an unshakable faith. If you are facing an impossible or hard situation in your life, faith allows you to put it in perspective. Instead of allowing your fear or reasoning to determine how you react, look at whatever "it" is through the lens of faith, kind of like

Shadrach, Meshach and Abednego did when facing death's door.

Their Story:
"Nebuchadnezzar said to them, "Is it true, Shadrach, Meshach, and Abednego that you refuse to serve my gods or to worship the gold statue I have set up? I will give you one more chance to bow down and worship the statue I have made when you hear the sound of the musical instruments. But if you refuse, you will be thrown immediately into the blazing furnace. And then what god will be able to rescue you from my power?" Shadrach, Meshach, and Abednego replied, "O Nebuchadnezzar, we do not need to defend ourselves before you. If we are thrown into the blazing furnace, the God whom we serve is able to save us. He will rescue us from your power, Your Majesty. But even if he doesn't, we want to make it clear to you, Your Majesty that we will never serve your gods or worship the gold statue you have set up."" - Daniel 3:14-18

Their faith in God was so solid that when put in a life or death situation they chose not to compromise, and were thrown into a fiery furnace. But before it led to what could have been a deadly situation, they said, "But even if he doesn't" Selah. King Nebuchadnezzar threw three men into the furnace, but when he looked up, four men were walking around inside of it. Nebuchadnezzar called the men out of the furnace. Noticing that they escaped untouched from the fire, he proclaimed God's greatness, and then promoted Shadrach, Meshach, and Abednego.

Do you have this kind of faith in God? How do you respond when God doesn't answer your prayers the way you think they should be solved? What do you do when God doesn't supernaturally intervene on your behalf? Does that make Him any less God? What do you do when you feel like God has failed you for one reason or another?

Maybe you are facing a crisis of belief, wondering why God hasn't stepped into your circumstances. Perhaps your faith is wavering in the midst of a situation that leaves you wondering, "Where is God and why hasn't He rescued you?" Maybe you are floundering in pain and anguish, wondering if you will ever serve the God you once loved and proclaimed. There is good news for you. Even if you don't have that "even if He doesn't" kind of faith right now, maybe your circumstances are designed to build the very faith you long for. Perhaps you are in the process of growing an even if He doesn't kind of faith. The truth is that this type of faith isn't built overnight.

Daniel and his friends made a decision when they were taken captive in Babylon, not to defile themselves with the rich foods of the Babylonians. They were committed to God, to follow His ways, and to live the way they had been taught from childhood. They didn't start building this type of faith when they arrived in Babylon; they had been growing it from their previous experiences with God and what they were taught as children.

This type of faith is built when we repeatedly choose God's ways over our own momentary pleasure. It's a faith that is formed by making a decision to walk according to God's ways.

Faith that says "even if He doesn't" is cultivated by God walking you through the trials of this life.

Shadrach, Meshach, and Abednego did not have an easy life. They were taken from their home in Jerusalem, living as captives in a foreign land. Because of the incredible wisdom God had given them, they were prime targets for others who were jealous. They had survived imprisonment and execution order.

Prayer: Like Shadrach, Meshach and Abednego may your faith and belief in God serve as your anchor as you face the challenges of life. I pray that your heart would be open to receiving the fullness of who God is and that His lordship will be established in your heart. May we be so rooted in our faith that those around us will see Jesus in the midst of our fire. May our light shine so brightly that all men and women we encounter will come to know that God is real. In Jesus name, Amen.

CHAPTER 7
FAITH MAKES YOU BOLD

#JustBelieve

"Faith isn't the ability to believe long and far into the misty future. It's simply taking God at His Word and taking the next step." - Joni Erickson Tada

Faith makes you bold. Have you ever desired to do something great, but were too afraid to see it through? This has been the story of my life. I've always desired to do great things, but either doubted if I could actually accomplish it. Passive personality's occasionally fall into this trap. They assume that faith is merely a quiet confidence in God that requires little to no activity on their part. Let's be honest when you think of a Christian, boldness is not the first attribute you think of to define one. If anything we think of scriptures that talk about forgiveness, meekness, and humility or flagship faith leaders who the world recognizes as the epitome of what a faith filled person should look like. Usually silent, meek, humble, and passive total pushovers.

I can't even begin to tell you the countless times people expected me to be passive when conflict or controversial issues arose. I'm glad to say, I disappointed them all. You probably have encountered these types of people that expected you to be like Mother Teresa, Nelson Mandela, or Dr. Martin Luther King Jr.

Mother Teresa was a sainted woman who founded the Missionaries of Charity a catholic organization that houses thousands of women and is active in over hundreds of countries. During the inauguration of her organization in the early 1950's she was a very controversial figure but was dedicated to wholeheartedly providing free services to the poorest of the poor at all cost. As a result of her faith convictions, her organization still provides care for people who are dying from terminal illness like AIDS, leprosy, cancer and various diseases. Until this day, her organization manages hundreds of soup kitchens, food pantries; dispensaries and mobile clinics; children's- and family counseling services; orphanages, and educational facilities.

The late Nelson Mandela who is and forever will be the ultimate definition of a freedom fighter was a lawyer and revolutionary political leader who served as the first Black President of South Africa from 1994 to 1999. Mandela was convicted, imprisoned and handed a life sentence for allegedly conspiring to overthrow the racist government that made racism legal through apartheid laws. He served twenty-seven years in prison, but after his release received a Nobel Peace Prize for his commitment to the unification of all of South Africa and the establishment of anti-apartheid laws and social norms for all people.

Out of all these amazing people, my personal favorite is the late Dr. Martin Luther King Jr. He was a small town country preacher who became the face of the Civil Rights Movement and President of the Southern Christian Leadership Conference who fought for the civil rights of Blacks in America through non-violence and civil disobedience. He became a worldwide figure for peace and racial reconciliation after he delivered his infamous "I Have A Dream" speech. Notice Mother Teresa, Mandela, and King all did great things that were all Nobel Peace Prize worthy, but were all motivated by their faith.

These amazing figures have been written in history as some of the world's greatest faith leaders. All three were motivated by their faith, but they were not weak they were bold. They did not hesitate to break unfair rules and societal boundaries that were unjust. In the face of calamity, confusion, racism, prejudice, death threats their faith empowered them to stand for what they believed under extreme pressure. It is under this type of pressure that our faith pushes us to become bold. 2 Timothy 1:7 say's that God has not given us a spirit of fear, but of power, love and a sound mind. God does not just call us to be humble and meek; this scripture proves that he has also given us the ability to be strong, powerful and bold. This is what I call Holy Boldness.

This is a type of boldness that isn't manufactured by the pride or achievements of man, but given directly from God as a tool to get work done. Acts 28: 31 shows us in order for the Apostles to spread the message of Jesus and expand the church they had to teach the word with boldness and without hindrance. Early in the New Testament in the book of Proverbs it's recorded that the wicked cowers when no one pursues, but the righteous are bold as a lion.

Believe it or not, Ephesians 3:12 say's, we as faith-filled Christians have boldness and access with confidence through our faith in Jesus. Mind blowing, I know. This is important to the modern believer because believing in Jesus does not mean your weak or have to put up with folks foolishness. I saw a shirt the other day that read, "I'm saved, not soft" though comical, it is truth. A faith-filled life is one that is filled with boldness to accomplish what you were put on earth to do. Often times, people wait for opportunities to fall in their lap or the right moment for things to happen for them, when really all they need is the boldness to step out and do what God has placed in their hearts.

What is in your heart to do in the world that you've been too afraid to accomplish? Have you allowed the fear of failure, stress, anxiety and the opinions of others to sow seeds of doubt and fear into your heart? If so, I want to begin to pray for boldness. I declare a holy boldness be your portion. In order to do what you have been put on this earth to do, it is going to require tough skin, perseverance, and a whole lot of prayer. You won't be able to accomplish it while living a life full of shame, rejection, and fear. I challenge you to cast away the fear that has been sent from hell to cripple your vision and faith. Dare to believe, dare to be bold.

One of the boldest moves I have ever made in my life was moving to Chicago to attend North Park University. I grew up in a small rural town where almost 50% of its students of color never made it past their sophomore year of high school. Most of the people of color from this city lived below the national poverty line. Needless to say, seeing an educated man of color, was very slim. Most of the men I grew up around worked low paying blue collar jobs and had very little education. I knew if I was going to do something different with my life, I was going to have to make a bold move.

Looking at the lives of people like Nelson Mandela, Martin Luther King, and Mother Teresa motivated me to step out on faith and believe I could do anything. At 18 years old with $1,000 dollars to my name I purchased a one way ticket to Chicago, packed two bags and moved to The Windy City. I honestly did not know what was going to happen. I strongly believed that God would take care of me. During this time, I adopted a new faith mantra that set the tone for my life and one that I use to this very day. *"God, if you don't do it, it won't be done."*

This is my way of quickly saying to the Lord that I'm depending on you to make it. I lived by and quoted Matthew 6:25-34 daily.

"Therefore I tell you, do not worry about your life, what you will eat or drink; or about your body, what you will wear. Is not life more than food, and the body more than clothes? Look at the birds of the air; they do not sow or reap or store away in barns, and yet your heavenly Father feeds them. Are you not much more valuable than they? Can any one of you by worrying add a single hour to your life ᵉ ? "And why do you worry about clothes? See how the flowers of the field grow. They do not labor or spin. Yet I tell you that not even Solomon in all his splendor was dressed like one of these. If that is how God clothes the grass of the field, which is here today and tomorrow is thrown into the fire, will he not much more clothe you— you of little faith? So do not worry, saying, 'What shall we eat?' or 'What shall we drink?' or 'What shall we wear?' For the pagans run after all these things, and your heavenly Father knows that you need them. But seek first his kingdom and his righteousness, and all these things will be given to you as well. Therefore do not worry about tomorrow, for tomorrow will worry about itself. Each day has enough trouble of its own.

It's been a remarkable 10 years since the journey here to the Windy City. Thankfully, I have an amazing family of my own and have had the privilege to touch thousands of lives for the glory of God. I wonder what would have happened if I allowed fear and the negative words of others keep me from doing what I felt in my heart was the will of God for my life.

Prayer: May the boldness and assurance that rested on Deborah in the bible rest on and in you. May it push you to break down strongholds and limitations that have been assigned to stunt your ability to see and believe beyond where you are. In Jesus name, Amen.

CHAPTER 8
FAITH CAN BE GROWN

#JustBelieve

"And where hope grows, miracles blossoms."- Elena Rae

In Hebrews 10:36-39, we are encouraged to stand on the promises of God. This is what turns hope into faith. There is this major misconception that faith in Jesus Christ is for some old lady who goes to church and chews on soft peppermints. I would beg to differ! Faith is a substance that our current and future generations need more than ever. It's the fundamental opportunity to believe in someone bigger than ourselves. Research proves that most violent crimes that happen in urban communities most of the times boils down to an individual having no hope. They lack the ability to see past their current reality. If they are poor they don't see the possibility having wealth. If they are sick they can't see themselves healed. Hopelessness is a rampart disease that has taken more lives than any gun or violent crime has. Don't just take my word for it look all around us our world is freaking crumbling. With issues like Police Brutality, Mass Incarceration, the Opioid Crisis, Terrorism, STD & STI rates, School Shootings, Racism, Sexism, Gang violence and Gun violence the world needs hope! When people have no hope they make hopeless decisions. Have you ever felt hopeless? As a result have you ever done anything that you're not proud of? The truth is we all have. Hope is so important because it speaks to the possibility of a better tomorrow.

Hope creates expectation that gives birth to unwavering faith. Hope say's there is a possibility for a better tomorrow, when faith say's not only do I think but I know and am sure that a better tomorrow is not going to come but it's already here.

Why is Living A Life of Faith So Hard?

Faith is every where. That's a bold headline. What I mean is that, faith is talked about in many places. Songs are written. Movies express overcoming obstacles when there seems to be no plan. There are tons of books on this subject. Finally, belief in the unseen is taught religiously, no pun intended, on most Sunday mornings.

So since this term is everywhere, why is it so challenging to live a life of faith?

One, we are not conscious.

Yes, we are alive and breathing. I mean that we are not aware. So how many times daily do you practice faith? We must change our awareness. Times of trouble, confusion, and doubt are an opportunity to practice what we already know to be true. We know that if we let go, just get out of the way, sit quietly, and give it to God, that our negative feelings will instantly be relieved. But, do we act this way? No. We try to solve it ourselves without the aid of the Lord. Then when this tactic makes things worse, we call on Him, but with a bone of where were you? In other words, we pray a prayer of pity. We haven't let go, we just shifted the blame. When you are in constant communication with God through reading His word and praying your request to God become personal.

Keys to Effective Faith

"Faith reaches into the realm of the spirit, grasps the promise of God and brings forth a tangible, physical fulfillment of that promise." - Gloria Copeland

Often, faith is weakened by a lack of faith-food. You may not be spending enough time studying and meditating on the Word of God. It's easy to let the cares and responsibilities of daily life crowd out time with God. Jesus taught as much in the parable of the sower. He said they choke the Word, and [faith] becomes unfruitful (Matthew 13:22). Faith needs to be nurtured, fed, and watered by the Word, in order to become strong and effective.

Sadly, most people won't do that. They'd rather hope that God will just 'fix it' - wave a magic wand, so to speak, and make it all better. Miracles do happen, but they are usually triggered by someone's faith. Everything God does on this earth is a result of faith and grace. Paul explained in Romans that it [whatever 'it' you are believing or hoping for] is of faith, that it might be given by grace [why?] so that the promise might be sure to all the seed (v. 4:16). The promise is 'sure', confirmed, absolute from God's side. Are you willing to do what it takes to develop your faith to make a strong connection?

One way to develop your faith is to recognize and acknowledge the good that is already present in your life. You need to know and admit that whatever good comes your way, it's from God. He's the Master behind it all. His good plan incorporates every good and perfect gift (James 1:17) - from the smallest to the greatest.

It's easy to get your thoughts tangled up in the negatives. Your whole body might feel just fine, but if you have a hangnail, the only thing you notice is the pain in your fingertip. In order for your faith to be effective, you need to focus on the positives and be eternally grateful. In every thing give thanks (1 Thessalonians 5:18). No matter what you're going through, find the good thing that you can be thankful for. Keeping your mind on things which are above (Colossians 3:2) is key to developing effective faith.

Just before He died on the cross, Jesus said, "It is finished." (John 10:30)What was? Everything He came to earth to do: to bring healing, deliverance, abundance, grace and mercy to every person. All He did during His earthly ministry would now carry forward into eternity. Old Testament verses that say 'shall' or 'will' became past tense with the death and resurrection of Christ! It is already done, as far as God is concerned.

You can have it all - every promise. Actually, you already have it- it is already in you! Jesus made the connection from heaven to earth. Now you need to use your faith to finish the connection.

Think of it this way. Electricity (power) is readily available at any outlet. But if you don't plug in the toaster or laptop, you won't have any power for your situation. No toast. No email.

Your faith 'communicates' with God, plugging in to the power of heaven. Study and meditate, then communicate your faith through prayer, praise, thanksgiving and declarations. Stay with it until your faith overpowers every faith blocker, hater every doubt and fear. Then you will experience results of effective faith and the fulfillment of every prayer.

3 Keys to Live a Life of Faith

Faith begins with you.

Sit back, relax, and enjoy these three keys that discuss how you can practice living a life of faith every day. Initially we have to reiterate what Faith is. Faith is a strong belief in an outcome that has yet to come. It's more than just positive thinking. Positive thinking involves your head. Faith goes deeper. Faith is knowing in your soul.

First Key: Begin thinking from the end.

Visualize the outcome that has yet to come. Imagery is more powerful than affirmation. Holding a picture in your mind is more powerful than uttering words. See words are thoughts. Words are not action. Visualization is picturing or placing yourself vividly in the outcome. Visualization is literally an action movie.

Remember the saying, seeing is believing? Change this expression to believing is seeing. All action is first conceived as a picture in the brain. Believe that it is true in your heart. See a clear picture of the outcome in your mind. The realization is on its way.

Second Key: Pray, Watch & Listen

Living a faith filled life has its challenges because we never know which way the current of life is going to take us. The Bible tells us that we should not only pray but watch as well. I'm not referring to physically watching, but watching by having our spirits in tuned with the Holy Spirit.

Step Three: Wait.

Patience is a virtue. Time gives us an opportunity to prepare ourselves. Sometimes we are not ready for what we want. Living a life of faith means trusting in the Lord, knowing that we live by His timetable not ours. This sometimes can be the most challenging thing because waiting is not always convenient.

CHAPTER 9
FAITH SPEAKS FROM A PREPARED PLACE

#JustBelieve

In one of the Triumph mentorship classes that I facilitate in a weekly dialogue, I had a revelation about faith. We were talking about the importance of having a plan and strategy for your life to ensure you have a road map to where you want to go. For most people, when creating a plan for their life, they tend not to know precisely where they want to be or only have a small idea of where they would like to accomplish.

As all of my mentees looked at me, by the way this was not a church or Christian environment, I realized that where we plan from is just as, if not more important, than the plan itself. How we plan and where we decide to build our lives from really matters. As believers, as we live our life it is imperative that we plan and build our lives from a place of faith. Throughout the Old and New Testament, we see an image of a loving God who loves his creation and calls us His children. Like a loving father, He ensures that our future is secure in Him. We see scriptures like Jeremiah 29:11 that says, "For I know the plans I have for you," declares the Lord, "plans to prosper you and not to harm you, plans to give you hope and a future," or Hebrews 11:1 which says, "Now faith is the assurance (title deed, confirmation) of things hoped for (divinely guaranteed), and the evidence of things not seen [the conviction of their reality—faith comprehends as fact what cannot be experienced by the physical senses]" I never realized that in context both speak to God's provision for His children.

Jeremiah alludes to the fact that God will be faithful to deliver His children in the midst of hardship and calamity. It assures the believer that as we go through life, crazy things will happen, but we have the assurance of knowing that God knows our end before our beginning and that through whatever happens in our life- suffering, chaos, sickness, or famine, that God has us. This assurance should allow us to stand firm in our faith knowing that God has already mapped out our victory in the midst of our pain and suffering.

"Weeping may endure for a night but joy comes in the morning (Psalm 30:5." This scripture informs us that our pain and suffering won't last forever. Rest assured it has an expiration date. Thus, this influences HOW we go through hard times. We know that it won't kill us, but will instead make us more aware of who and whose we are in Him.

As I was teaching the workshop to my students, I realized that faith is the bridge and the currency that is needed to manifest what only exists in faith to our natural everyday world. The thing is, whatever your dream or vision is for your life, you've already experienced it. If your vision is to start an ice cream business then before it ever materializes, and before you take out a loan or rent a building, you've already seen and experienced what it will look like in your mind.

The challenge will be to take the vision/ dream out of the realm of your imagination and manifest it into your reality. But you wouldn't be able manifest it, if you didn't see and experience it first from within. Faith is the tool and bridge needed to take what you see from within and bring it into the realm of reality. In short, don't pursue your life goals aimlessly. Know that before you were created, your purpose existed and it is waiting for you to wake up and have the faith and courage to pursue it.

Matthew 17:20 says, "I tell you the truth, if you have faith as small as a mustard seed, you can say to this mountain, 'Move from here to there' and it will move. Nothing will be impossible for you."

We can apply this to our lives every day. The mountain is not really a mountain. It can be any obstacle or problem you have in your life - debt, illness, loneliness, addictions, or more. If you believe that you deserve ONLY good things, KNOW that they will come as soon as you have faith.

Praying, reading the Bible and spending time in the presence of God are the best ways to grow your faith. Everybody has his/her own way to pray. You can pray aloud, in silence, singing, meditating, dancing, following a prayer, or silently. When you pray, you are talking with God. This is the best time to gain access to God's heart and learn about who He is through faith. Most people attempt to use faith as a slot machine that they use when they are willing to take a gamble on God because it's convenient. Others talk to the

Lord when they are in trouble and have nowhere else to turn. The good thing is that God does not play favorites, He rains on the just and the unjust and chooses to acknowledge the cries of His children.

Faith is the spiritual strand of DNA in every believer that connects them to the heavenly father. Faith is what connects our hearts to His it is what makes healing, deliverance, breakthrough, intimacy even salvation a reality in our lives. Most of all it connects us to each other. Yes, our faith in God makes us family.

Faith has the crazy ability to supernaturally connect you to a worldwide network of people who have encountered the love of Abba and have chosen to believe in Him. Isn't that crazy! For people like me who come from a broken family this is good news because you will never be alone. As a result of your faith you will always be connected to the family of God.

As I mentioned in a previous chapter I didn't grow up knowing my biological father and that caused great gaps in my soul. I never felt whole or fulfilled and always wondered what would my life be like if he was there? I consistently asked myself would my journey into manhood be as difficult if my father was there to coach me through the tough and hard seasons in my life. Today I can honestly say I would not be the man, father, husband, or son I am if it wasn't for the spiritual uncles, mothers, cousins, brothers, mentors, and fathers who took me in as family to help me along my journey.

Prior to having my own family I have lived with ten different families in various parts of the world, normally they knew very little about my story but because of our joining belief in Jesus they took a chance on me and let me physically stay in their homes. Some of my greatest life lessons were learned being around people who were not blood relatives but were connected to me through faith. The Apostle Paul author of most of the New Testament writes in Romans 8:14 -16 that those who are led by the Spirit of God are the children of God. The Spirit you received does not make you slaves, so that you live in fear again; rather, the Spirit you received brought about your adoption to son ship. *f* And by him we cry, "*Abba,* *g* Father."

The Spirit himself testifies with our spirit that we are God's children. Now if we are children, then we are heirs— heirs of God and co-heirs with Christ, if indeed we share in his sufferings in order that we may also share in his glory. In other words, in my most country voice, We family, Y'all.

CONCLUSION

This entire book has been laced with stories and a number of reasons why your faith matters. In the process, I have shared my heartaches, disappointments, failures, and a host of other challenges. The challenges have all pointed to why I should not have faith in Jesus.

Throughout my life, I've asked God the hard questions. God, if you love me why did you allow me to be sexually abused as a young boy? If you loved me, why did you allow me to grow up without my biological father? If you're such a good God, why didn't you prevent my wife from miscarrying? If you're such a good God, why does my mother suffer from memory loss due to multiple strokes?

Maybe you are like me, and have a list of your own questions to ask God about. The truth is, belief in God is the only way to begin to even unpack why things happen in the world. Pain and suffering was never part of God's original plan for His children. Yet, it is the result of a broken and fallen world caused by the poor, sinful, and selfish decisions of humans who God entrusted to manage His creation called earth.

When God created the world, inclusive of humans, the primary objective was for Him to love us and we love Him in return. Today, this is still God's primary objective. It was our sin that caused the divide from God our creator. This divide was the very thing that made Jesus's pain and suffering necessary. Pain and suffering slipped through the backdoor of our disobedience and open defiance to God's original plan for us. Am I saying that everyone who suffers deserves what they are getting? No. God is not some sick or twisted person who benefits from the pain of His children according to 2 Peter 3:9.

The bible describes God as loving, compassionate, merciful, patient and just. God does not have thunderbolts in His hand waiting to strike humanity down every time we make a decision that displeases or disappoints Him. He's a loving Father who wipes the tears from His children's eyes. He's the loving Father that never misses an important moment in the lives of His children. He's an attentive Father that daily counts the strands of hair on His children's head. He ensures that the righteous are never forsaken and that all of their needs are met.

God is the one that continues to keep the earth in orbit, but ensures that we are never scorched by the rays of the sun. He is the one who sent His only son to die to restore and redeem humanity back to himself to ensure that sin and death would not have the ability to ravish us. This is the same God that walked into hell and took the keys of sin and death to guarantee our abundant fulfilled life in Him. God does not glory in our sufferings, but on the contrary, since the beginning of time, He has relentlessly pursued us and is longing to be in relationship with His us.

God's track record is perfect. He is perfect, and He is good. Most of us have heard this sentiment, but have you ever really considered what God's faithfulness has cost Him? I'll tell you everything. John 3:16 records that, "God so loved the world that He gave His only beloved son so that whoever would believe in Him would not perish but have the opportunity to enjoy an abundant and everlasting life." The truth is that God is constantly reaching out for His children in hopes that we would love Him at least a fraction of how much He loves us. He waits patiently for us to respond to His love with obedience and sacrifice while we continue to enjoy things that continue to strengthen the divide between Him and us. We then treat Him like a side-chick or a lady of the night but expect martial benefits and blessings. Any healthy love relationship requires sacrifice. It requires a giving up of oneself and a crucifixion of one's will and desires so that relationship can flourish. The bible says that in order to be called a disciple of Christ we must be willing to deny ourselves and pick up our cross and follow Jesus.

Matthew 16:24- 26 says, Then Jesus told his disciples, "If anyone would come after me, let him deny himself and take up his cross and follow me. For whoever would save his life will lose it, but whoever loses his life for my name sake will find it. For what will it profit a man if he gains the entire world and forfeits his soul? Or what shall a man give in return for his soul?" True faith in Christ costs! Most social Christians believe God is some magic genie that grants any wish and fulfills any self-indulgent prayer that makes them happy. News flash, FAITH DOESN'T WORK LIKE THAT.

In many western countries, individuals are misinformed and believe that faith in Jesus will lead to a massive amount of wealth and riches. Once again, FAITH DOESN'T WORK LIKE THAT.

Many who have publicly professed their faith in Christ have paid a hefty price. Some have lost wealth, family, friends, children, spouses and in some extreme cases their life. I bring this up because often times we think about what God hasn't but negate what we haven't done. Ask yourself, do you only call on God when you're in trouble? When was the last time that your belief in God caused you to give up something you felt like you deserved? When is the last time your faith cost you something? When was the last time you picked up your cross to follow Jesus? Faith is not for the faint of heart.

Being a true disciple of Jesus requires you to pick up and carry a cross. This is a requirement not an option. The Bible uses the word 'faith' and its derivatives almost 350 times. While Old Covenant talks about God's faithfulness, the New Covenant shifts from His faith to ours. The entire New Testament shows us how Jesus walked by faith and how we are to learn to live by faith. If we look at the lives of the disciples, we quickly realize that faith is not for the weak. Most of Christ disciples were persecuted for their faith and spent time in prison for it. The crazy thing is the Church continued to grow. Today you and other believers around the world enjoy the benefits of a personal relationship with Jesus because of the dedicated people that encountered Jesus centuries ago and made a decision to believe out loud. What legacy is your faith leaving? Will generations to come be able to see the goodness of Jesus through your beliefs? Will the love and mercy of God be seen through your life or is your faith timid and tucked away? Believe out loud! Let your faith be seen and heard so that the world may see and know that Jesus is real.

One of the most robust instructions regarding faith was given to Joshua after Moses' death. Joshua was one of the twelve who were sent to spy out the Promised Land. After God told the Israelites that He had given them the land, only two, Joshua and Caleb, agreed with God's Word. The other ten came back complaining that the task was too difficult and the tribes of Israel could never win. They doubted God's Word, giving it no credit at all. They were faint of heart.

Forty years later, after Moses' death, it fell to Joshua to complete the task God had given the Israelites four decades earlier. Everyone in the previous generation was dead.

Their complaining and doubting had shortened their lives. Only Joshua and Caleb remained to lead the people. Here's what God told him, "Only be strong and very courageous, that you mayest observe to do according to all the law, which Moses My servant commanded you. Turn not from it to the right hand or to the left, so that you may prosper wherever you go (Joshua 1:7)." We can learn a lot from this instruction.

Faith believes.

Your faith and belief in God are vital not just for you, but also for those who may be transformed and or impacted by it! Never take how you live your life in front of co- workers, family, friends and even strangers for granted. A famous writer once said, "You May be the only Bible that someone will read and you may be the only Jesus some people may ever see (Unknown)." I urge you to think about this and think about the effects of your beliefs have on others. God doesn't ask us to have a lot of faith but to have faith the size of a grain of a mustard seed.

Part of picking up our cross is laying down or reframing how we view and interact with the world that we live in.

Jesus taught that we live in this world but are not of it. There was a powerful movement in the mid 90's called the What Would Jesus Do movement? This was a Christian social movement that became a popular motto amongst Christians around the world served as a reminder and a call for Christians to be intentional to act in a way that personified Jesus's teachings. The big idea was to shape lens and worldview in which believers essentially viewed the world and interacted through the eyes of Jesus. Thus effecting their moral, ethical, financial, and political compasses despite what their personal understanding or convictions were. I believe this is the way that we honor God with our life and allow our faith to flourish in our post Christian world. We choose to actively lay down what we think for what He said about it.

The Christ centered worldview is based on the sovereignty and divinity of God and His written word. As Christians we believe God has given us the bible as a set of instructions on how to live in the world until His return. This may sound extreme to some, but the essence of the Christian life is one of sacrifice.

We stand with scripture and believe that every ounce of it is inspired and breathed out of the heart and mouth of God and profitable for teaching, reproof, for correction, and for training in righteousness. 2 Timothy 3:16-17

If this is not the case we will be like everyone else in and of the world trying to search for objectivity in a sea of subjectivity.

Every bit of this literary work has been guided by the Holy Spirit. Just Believe was written to inspire, invoke and ignite a culture of life-giving faith around the world. I would like for you to consider inviting/hosting our ministry this upcoming year to help us fulfill the mandate the Lord has given us to create opportunities for the voice of God to be heard and His love demonstrated and for our new ministry resource to be put into the hands of the next generation. The premise of this book is to serve as a resource for the next generation to have an understanding of why it is important for us to believe in Jesus. In my professional career as an educator, mentor, and professor I see the effects the next generations god-lessness thus am aware of the urgency to create spaces where the next generation can encounter the love and presence of God for themselves. More than ever in times like this when the media, worldly systems, and modern culture attempt to discredit and damage the reputation of Jesus and His church we need to be charged and reminded why our faith in Jesus matters.

In Judges 2:10 says that after the death of Joshua and those who had seen God's mighty acts, "there arose another generation after them, who did not know the Lord or the work which he had done for Israel." And the result of this ignorance "The people of Israel did what was evil in the sight of the Lord and served the Baals; and they forsook the Lord, the God of their fathers, who had brought them out of the land of Egypt."

The three lessons for us that I want to draw out of this text are simple but so necessary.

First, when the knowledge of God is preserved in our communities, especially by those who have personally experienced God's power, faith is nourished and obedience flourishes.

Second, if we allow the next generation to grow up without this knowledge of God, we serve not only their ignorance and unbelief but also their destruction.

Third, therefore it is our solemn duty to teach and demonstrate the fullness of who God is so that the next generation will believe and be saved.

REFERENCES

Chapter 3

What is your excuse? Christian 12 Step
https://www.christian12step.org/what-is-your-excuse/

Chapter 5

https://www.gotquestions.org/what-happens-death.html
https://www.alustforlife.com/mental-health/well
being/forgiveness-is-for-you-not-anyone-else
https://www.watchmanmin.org.au/soul-ties-trauma-bonds/).

51993044R00069

Made in the USA
Columbia, SC
25 February 2019